Friends of the Library
Used Book Store
Serendipity Corner
553 S. Maine

SHIPS OF COMMERCE

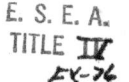

Liners, Tankers, Freighters, Tugboats,
Floating Grain Elevators

by C. B. Colby

Coward, McCann & Geoghegan   New York

This historic photo shows a later version of the Clermont, Robert Fulton's first steam-powered craft, scoffingly called "Fulton's Folly." Note the masts and furled sails in case the steam engine failed. For many years steamboats carried both engines and sails, until steam power proved reliable.

Contents

Ships of Commerce	3
SS *United States* (passenger liner)	4
SS *America* (passenger liner)	6
SS *Constitution* (passenger liner and cruise ship)	8
SS *Atlantic* (cruise ship)	9
T/V *Leonardo da Vinci* (passenger liner)	10
SS *Excalibur* (combination passenger and freighter)	11
SS *Canberra*, SS *Orsova* and SS *Iberia* (passenger liners)	12
SS *France* (passenger liner)	14
SS *Queen Elizabeth* and SS *Queen Mary* (passenger liners)	15
Peter Stuyvesant (excursion steamer)	16
Delta Queen (excursion steamer)	17
Circle Line XII (sightseeing boats)	18
Miss New York (ferryboat)	19
Export Courier (freighter)	20
Export Ambassador (freighter)	21
Alcoa Puritan, Esparta, Cartago and Tilapa (freighters)	22
American Challenger (freighter)	24
SS *Elizabethport* (container freighter)	26
Seatrain Georgia (railway car and container carrier)	28
M/V Harry Jefferies and J. E. Dyer (oil tankers)	30
Amoco Wisconsin and SS Meadowbrook (oil tankers)	32
SS *Cobetas* (grain carrier) and Floating Grain Elevators	34
Albatross IV, George M. Bowers and M/V Delaware (research)	36
John N. Cobb, Oregon and Kaho (fishing research)	38
Diana L. Moran (tugboat)	40
United States, Philip Sporn and Patrick Calhoun, Jr. (towboats)	42
Dredges	44
Barges	46

Photo Credits

The Port of New York Authority: title page, 10, 14, 26, 27, 31, 34, 35, 41, 46, 47 center and bottom, 48; New York Historical Society, New York City: 2; United States Lines: full color cover transparency and 4, 5, 6, 7, 24, 25; American Export Lines: 8, 9, 11, 20, 21; P & O Orient Lines, Inc.: 12, 13; Cunard Steamship Co., Ltd.: 15; Hudson River Day Line: 16; Greene Line Steamers, Inc.: 17; Circle Line: 18; New York City Department of Marine and Aviation: 19; Alcoa Steamship Co.: 22; United Fruit Co.: 23; Seatrain Lines, Inc.: 28, 29; Sinclair Refining Co.: 30, 47 top; Moran Towing and Transportation Co., Inc.: 31 bottom, 40; Keystone Shipping Co.: 32 lower; American Oil Co.: 32 top, 33; U. S. Fish and Wildlife Service: 36, 37, 38, 39; Federal Barge Lines, Inc.: 42, 43 top; American Barge Lines Co.: 43 center and lower; Ellicott Machine Corp.: 44, 45.

Copyright © 1963 by C. B. Colby   All rights reserved.   Manufactured in the United States of America

Library of Congress Catalog Card Number: 63-15539

Sixth Impression

SBN: GB 698-30312-1

Ships of Commerce

Since more than two-thirds of the earth is covered with water, it seems only natural that interest in ships and shipping is so widespread. Whether a person lives on the coast or far inland, his life is affected in many ways by ships of commerce, from his own and other lands.

The economy of every country with a seacoast, navigable rivers or freshwater inland seas or lakes is affected by her ships, her shipping and her mariners. Her ships may ply only among her own ports, or sail the seven seas in trade, but no matter where they go, their effect is far-reaching and their goings and comings are exciting and fun to watch.

There are hundreds of different types of boats, vessels and ships, some so highly specialized that they are seldom seen. There are others whose silhouettes are well known around the globe. There are harbor craft that never venture onto the high seas; riverboats that never reach the coast of their own country; and great inland lake steamers, larger than many a seagoing craft, whose hulls have never touched salt water. There are "coasters" that travel from coastal port to coastal port, seldom out of sight of land, and "tramps" that travel the globe picking up cargoes and passengers where they can find them, with no particular schedule or ports of call. Great luxury liners make scheduled runs across the oceans with the regularity of trains or planes; gay tourist ships ply the warm waters of the tropics in leisurely escape from the winters of the north. Research vessels chart the oceans and their depths for the markets of the world.

Some ships are as luxurious as the finest resort hotels, while others are as businesslike as battleships. Modern shipping lines are becoming more and more considerate of the comfort of the crews as well as the passengers, with good quarters, air conditioning and really fine food. The sailors of today have a far better lot than the "iron men" of yesterday, who went to sea in wooden ships with little comfort.

On the following pages you will see a wide variety of ships from lakes, rivers, harbors and the open sea. Some are luxurious, some strictly for work and some just for fun. All are in business, big business, for they are the world's ships of commerce.

I have selected outstanding examples of ocean liners, harbor tugs, freighters, boats of inland waterways, famous river and excursion steamers, and some offbeat types just for their unusual interest. Some types are traditional and even legendary, and some as modern as a spaceship.

The ships I have selected may be found in almost identical types on similar waters around the globe, with some minor alterations because of local conditions or preferences. A tug in any harbor must have the same basic lines and characteristics to operate efficiently. A luxury liner, no matter what flag she flies or where her home port may be, must compete with others in the same business and offer as much in passenger comfort and luxury as the next. Freighters of all flags must carry the most cargo possible with the greatest economy of fuel, at the fastest possible speed. Their design must be of proven efficiency. Therefore the ships you will find as you turn these pages could be flying the flag of almost any nation.

I am sure you will find many famous ships among them, whose names you have heard and read many times. You will also find names and types you have never known about, unless you have lived near the water where they go about their business, or are as fond of ships as I am.

Ever since I earned my "lifeboat ticket" and was handed my seaman's passport nearly forty years ago, I have been thrilled by the harbor sights and sounds of many ports. Perhaps in reading this book and seeing these ships of many seas and rivers, you too will decide that there is something special about the life of a sailor.

I must express my appreciation for the enthusiastic help of many fine folks in the marine shipping industry in obtaining the outstanding photos for this book. In particular I would like to thank Mr. Myron L. Hurwitz of The Port of New York Authority for his very great help. Without such fine cooperation many of these outstanding photos would have been impossible to locate and obtain. My thanks to all who lent a hand.

— C. B. COLBY

SS United States *(passenger liner)*

Winner of the Hales Trophy for the fastest crossing of the Atlantic Ocean, between Ambrose Lightship off the coast of New York and Bishop's Rock off the coast of England, in both directions, the SS *United States* is the new speed champion of the seas. This United States Lines passenger liner was the first American ship to win this Atlantic Blue Riband speed trophy in almost one hundred years. Her time eastbound was three days, ten hours and forty minutes at an average speed of 35.59 knots. Her westbound time was three days, twenty hours and forty-two minutes at an average speed of 30.99 knots. By contrast, the *Mayflower* took over two months for her crossing, and weighed 180 tons compared with the 53,300 tons of this great ship. The *United States* is 990 feet long (nearly five city blocks), and the only wood aboard is in the grand pianos and the butcher's chopping block. Her crew includes 1,050 officers and men and she can carry approximately 1,750 passengers, or 2,000 in an emergency. Her beam (width) is over 100 feet and she can travel 10,000 miles without stopping for fuel, water or food. She carries 22 nonsinkable type lifeboats, which can carry 3,000 persons. She is as tall as a 12-story building (175 feet from keel to top of stacks) and her theater alone can seat over 350 people. There are kennels for pets, complete hospital and operating room and 18 elevators. Photo above shows SS *United States* at sea, while opposite page (top) shows first-class suite, and (lower) first-class dining room. There are garages for passenger cars, children's play areas, gift shops and ballrooms. She is equipped with every type of navigation and safety device as well as radios, and is completely air-conditioned. Truly a magnificent ship to carry the Stars and Stripes. This is the liner shown in full color on the cover.

SS America (passenger liner)

This sister ship of the SS *United States* is slightly smaller but no less luxurious for her passengers. She is 723 feet in length and her beam is 93 feet. She carries an average passenger list of just under a thousand but can carry considerably more if need be. She, like her sister ship, is equipped with the latest in safety and navigation equipment, and her lifeboats can carry more persons than she would normally have aboard under any circumstances. She has shops, a hospital, theater, ballroom, play decks, children's areas and every convenience for the passengers. At the top is shown SS *America* underway and, below, a view of the smoking room. On the opposite page (top) a view of one of her dining rooms, and (bottom) the beautifully appointed lounge. These views look more like those of a hotel than the interior of a ship. Her cabins are equally well equipped and decorated. This United States Lines transatlantic passenger ship, like the SS *United States*, is one of the finest luxury liners afloat.

SS Constitution *(passenger liner and cruise ship)*

This aerial view shows the sleek SS *Constitution* of the American Export Lines, a smaller passenger ship than those on preceding pages, but a luxury liner designed for the complete comfort of the tourist. She is 683 feet long with a beam of 89 feet. She has a top speed of over 26 knots and can carry 1,088 passengers. She and her identical sister ship, the SS *Independence*, are designed so that passengers can find almost anything for their pleasure from dancing to swimming pools (each ship has two). The fine theater seats about 150 and there is plenty of deck space for ping-pong, shuffleboard, deck tennis and sunbathing. Note the 14 lifeboats hung on davits, the two swimming pools and the rows of deck chairs for sunning on the aft deck. The various king posts (short "masts"), on the forward and aft decks, and their booms are for handling light cargo and supplies. The mast forward carries the various radar devices and antennas for the radios. In some ships the huge funnels are not always used as smokestacks, but for storage, with only a small inner stack carrying the smoke.

SS Excalibur (combination passenger and freighter)

One of the most popular types of ships for the tourist is the combination passenger and freighter, such as American Export Lines SS *Excalibur*. Her regular runs carry her to Europe and the Mediterranean, and she can carry 124 passengers in exceptional comfort along with about 5,000 tons of cargo. Although her passenger accommodations are more limited than on a straight passenger ship, they are all first class and the ship boasts fine dining rooms, lounges, a swimming pool and complete passenger-accommodation air conditioning. (There is a sister ship, the SS *Exeter*, almost identical.) This photo shows the port side of the ship. Note the many king posts and booms for cargo handling, as well as the foremast and mainmast. Note also radar atop mast just forward of funnel. The combining of cargo and passenger handling in one ship gives the passengers the opportunity to witness the exciting and complicated business of loading and unloading a wide variety of cargo at many ports. The length of these sister ships is 473 feet, with a beam of 66 feet. Their speed is about 17 knots and their tonnage 14,893 tons. The small passenger list enables travelers to get to know each other quickly, and all enjoy one class of service.

SS Canberra, SS Orsova and SS Iberia
(passenger liners)

This passenger ship of the P&O Orient Lines Pacific Fleet has many unusual features besides its unusual appearance. The SS *Canberra* is the largest passenger ship in the Pacific and can carry more passengers than almost any other ship afloat. She can carry 2,238 passengers and a crew of 1,000, made possible by the fact that her superstructure is the largest all-aluminum structure of its kind in the world. This light structure allows for the addition of an extra deck to accommodate more passengers. The twin funnels indicate that the engine rooms are aft, leaving the widest center part of the ship free for passengers. Engine vibration and noise are behind the passengers rather than under them. Cargo handling through the ship's side has eliminated topside loading king posts and booms. Even automobiles can be loaded through the side by a conveyor. This interesting ship is 820 feet long, with a beam of 102 feet and has a speed of over 27 knots. She is equipped with a transverse propulsion system which permits her to move sideways; a great aid in docking. On opposite page (top) is the SS *Orsova* and (bottom) the SS *Iberia*, both of the same fleet. The *Orsova* is 722 feet long with a 93-foot beam and a speed of 22 knots. She carries 1,494 passengers and a crew of 634. The SS *Iberia* is 720 feet long with a beam of 90 feet and a speed of 22 knots. She carries 1,410 passengers and a crew of 711. There are 14 ships in this fleet of passenger carriers.

SS France (passenger liner)

This beautiful photo shows the SS France of the French Line being welcomed to New York after her maiden voyage in 1962. This is the longest passenger liner afloat, with a length of 1,035 feet and a beam of 110 feet. She has a speed in excess of 30 knots. She carries 2,000 passengers and a crew of over 1,200. She is filled with many of the "largest" items of any ship. For example, she has the largest theater with a capacity of 664; the largest floating dining room which can seat 800 at a single meal; the two longest covered promenade decks, each measuring 341 feet; and the longest bar afloat. She also has the largest children's play area on any passenger liner. Besides passengers she also carries considerable cargo. One unusual feature of the SS France is the unique "soot catchers" on either side of the funnel tops, which are designed to prevent particles of black soot from her engines from falling on the passengers below. Everything for passenger comfort is included in this great French Line ship. Note the two helicopters circling the ship, one in lower left-hand corner of photo and one just over the stern.

SS Queen Elizabeth and SS Queen Mary
(passenger liners)

No book on ships would be complete without including the "Queens." At top is shown the huge SS *Queen Elizabeth*, 1,031 feet long with a gross tonnage of 83,673 tons and a speed of 28.5 knots. She can carry 2,300 passengers. The lower photo shows her sister queen, the SS *Queen Mary*, with a length of 1,019 feet and a gross tonnage of 81,237 tons. She can carry 2,040 passengers. Both of these ships are luxury liners in every sense of the word and have carried many hundreds of thousands of passengers across the Atlantic. Built in 1940 and completed after the war started, the *Queen Elizabeth* was immediately put into service as a troopship and carried many thousands of troops across the North and South Atlantic. The *Queen Mary*, completed in 1936, also saw much service during the war. Both are now in service for the famed Cunard Steamship Co., Ltd.

Peter Stuyvesant *(excursion steamer)*

Every summer thousands of vacationers, tourists and "holidayers" board huge river excursion boats for a few hours of sun, fun and relaxation. Such rivers as the Hudson, in New York State, offer fine excursions for many miles. The Hudson River Day Line operates veteran steamers such as the *Peter Stuyvesant* shown above. This great pleasure craft can carry 2,777 passengers and is operated by a crew of 26. She is 270 feet long and has a speed of around 18 knots. Excursion "boats" of this type are really far too large to be classified as a boat, but over the years, since the time when excursions were usually taken on much smaller craft, the name has remained. When a boat is so large that it cannot normally be carried aboard another vessel, it is usually referred to as a ship or vessel. Such river steamers as this feature sun decks, music, often a lecturer to point out sights along the way, and unlimited numbers of hot dogs and hamburgers, not to mention soda and popcorn. Excursions on these river steamers are often the only cruises possible for thousands of folks, and they fill a great need for fun and sun during the summer months.

Delta Queen (excursion steamer)

Who has not heard of the historic Mississippi River stern-wheelers, the showboats and excursion boats and all the romantic tales about them? They are almost a vanishing "species" of steamboat, but at least one is still going strong and its popularity as a different kind of vacation cruise ship is increasing. The photo shows this romantic craft, the *Delta Queen*, which cruises up and down the Ohio, Mississippi and Tennessee rivers from March to November. It is operated by Greene Line Steamers, Inc., of Cincinnati, Ohio, and aboard her you can recapture a lot of the fun and excitement of the "sternwheelers" of yesterday. One of her outstanding features is a steam calliope which plays tunes along the way, as in the days of the old showboats. The *Delta Queen* is 285 feet long, can carry up to 200 passengers plus a crew of 76. Her great paddle wheel of steel and wood measures 28 feet in diameter and is painted bright red. She is air-conditioned and features southern cooking, plenty of square dancing and other entertainment, besides the legendary riverboat atmosphere. The cruises can last as long as 20 days, and I'm sure even Mark Twain would have enjoyed them.

Circle Line XII *(sightseeing boats)*

A smaller type of excursion craft is the sightseeing boat, usually used in short cruises about inland waters. Typical of this type of boat, but not typical of the backgrounds for most of them, are the yachts used by the Circle Line of New York City. These were all former landing craft, and many of them saw action in the Pacific during World War II. They have been converted into safe, spacious and dependable sightseeing boats. They are 180 feet long and have a speed of 15 knots. They carry 600 passengers and a crew of about nine. Besides the captain, mate, engineer and deckhands, there is a lecturer who points out all the interesting sights of New York as the yacht makes its trip around the island of Manhattan. In the photo above she is shown passing the famed Statue of Liberty, which appears to be riding the top-deck roof. She has plenty of seats for all, enclosed as well as open areas, and these yachts can ride out really rough weather if need be.

Miss New York (ferryboat)

One of the busiest of all ships of commerce is the ferryboat. All cities situated on big rivers or even along the coasts of countries require the services of ferries, often several in operation at once. The photo above shows one of the many ferries in operation about the great harbor of New York. These ferries are operated by the Department of Marine and Aviation of the city, or under this department's supervision. In one year nearly twenty-five million passengers and almost two million cars were carried on one of the several lines alone, not to mention the mileage covered, which totaled 323,950 miles for this same run. There are five different ferry services in New York City. The average ferry is 290 feet long and can carry more than 2,000 passengers and up to 45 cars. Some are larger and some are smaller than the *Miss New York* shown above. She can carry 2,328 passengers and 26 cars. The speed of these ferries is about 17 knots. They carry crews of up to 13. They are equipped with radar, ship-to-shore radio phones and many safety devices. Note the duplicate pilothouses on each end. The pilot merely walks to the other pilothouse for the return trip and starts back without having to turn the ferry around. Passengers and vehicles can load and disbark from either end. These ferries are important to commuter travel into and out of the city.

Export Courier (freighter)

There are many types of freighters or cargo ships, some designed to handle general cargo, some specific types of cargo. The photo above shows the Export Courier, of the American Export Lines, which has a length of 493 feet and a beam of 73 feet. She has a top speed of better than 18 knots and is equipped with all the latest cargo-handling facilities. For example, the big hatch covers are hydraulically operated and the six holds have a general cargo capacity of 731,548 cubic feet. The many booms for handling cargo are located for maximum efficiency, and on one hatch there is an extra-heavy boom with a capacity of 60 tons. No quarters are provided for passengers on this ship, which is designed strictly for cargo, but she does have fine, air-conditioned accommodations for 54 officers and crew. Note that the Export Courier is what is known as an engine-aft design, with the power plant and stack in the stern. The bridge and some of the quarters are amidships, as you can see by the long row of bridge windows. She is equipped with all latest navigation and communications equipment.

Export Ambassador *(freighter)*

Here is another American Export Lines freighter, with a completely different silhouette, and with the engines amidships. This freighter has a length of 492 feet, a beam of 73 feet and a speed of 18 knots. She has room for 12 passengers and a crew of 54 officers and men. The hatch covers are hydraulically controlled, and she is equipped to handle a wide variety of cargo. The six cargo holds have 553,511-cubic-foot bale capacity, plus 24,037 cubic feet of refrigerated space, 51,628 cubic feet of liquid-cargo capacity and special cargo rooms totaling 17,860 cubic feet. She is fitted with deep tanks with high-speed pumps for handling bulk liquids and semi-liquids. Temperature and humidity can be controlled to minute accuracy to help preserve many types of delicate cargo. Her booms can handle loads up to 50 tons with their powerful electric winches. Note the small stream of smoke from the actual funnel inside the large dummy stack. She is equipped with radar (atop mast over the bridge) and the latest in navigation and safety equipment.

Alcoa Puritan, Esparta, Cartago and Tilapa (freighters)

Among all the various types and sizes of freighters, you will see a wide variety of king post and cargo boom arrangements. Here are four different engine-amidship freighters with as many different arrangements of cargo-handling derricks, all designed to make handling of cargo for that particular ship fast and efficient. At the top is the *Alcoa Puritan* of the Alcoa Steamship Company. She is 417 feet long and has a beam of 60 feet and a speed of about 15 knots. On the opposite page are three typical freighters of the "Great White Fleet" of the United Fruit Company. At the top is the *Esparta*, with a length of 431 feet, a beam of 61 feet and a speed of about 18 knots. Middle photo shows the *Cartago*, and at the bottom is the *Tilapa*. Both of these are slightly smaller in gross tonnage than the *Esparta*. The *Esparta* has a gross tonnage of 7,075 tons, the *Cartago* a gross tonnage of 6,797 tons and the *Tilapa* a gross tonnage of 6,738 tons. Note the variety of booms and king posts in these four freighters.

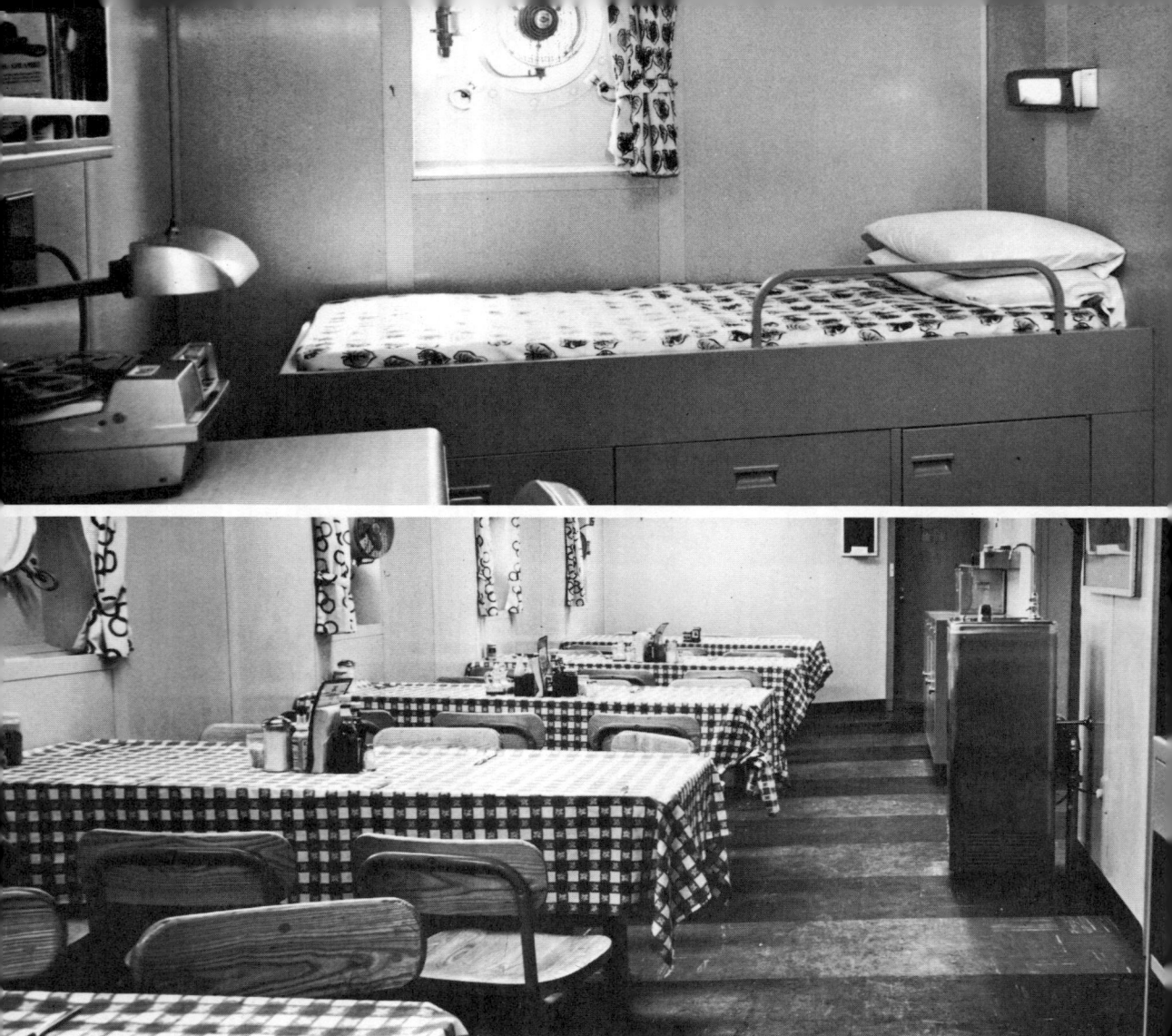

American Challenger (freighter)

This modern-type freighter of the United States Lines holds several speed records and is typical of the new look in freighters. She is 560 feet long and has a beam of 75 feet. Her speed is better than 21 knots. She is able to carry 580,102 cubic feet of dry cargo, a refrigerated cargo of 45,130 cubic feet, plus another 45,673 cubic feet of additional cargo, for a total of 670,905 cubic feet, all easily reached via modern cargo-handling equipment. Huge containers for complete manufacturer-to-customer delivery without opening can be handled on a door-to-door basis with ease. Refrigerated cargoes are protected with precisely controlled temperature equipment and a complete air change every hour. The powerful booms (one with a capacity of 70 tons) assure fast and safe handling of anything the ship can accommodate. The quarters for the officers and crew are particularly modern. Above is a photo of one of the cabins and below this a shot of the pleasant dining room. On the opposite page is an unusual bow-on aerial view of this modern-day freighter. Note the clean lines of the bow and the clean deck areas with a minimum of rigging, cables and cargo-handling equipment. A ship in the finest American tradition, this is the freighter on the cover.

SS *Elizabethport* (container freighter)

To help speed cargo from portal to portal, a whole new system of freight movement was designed. Giant vans mounted on truck trailer beds can be loaded, sealed and then shipped "without wheels" to another part of the coast or another country, replaced on wheels and hauled to the destination. The ships designed for this unique means of freight or cargo delivery are indeed unusual. Here is the SS *Elizabethport*, operated by Sea-Land Service, Inc. She is 630 feet long with a beam of 78 feet. There are 45 in the crew and she has a speed of 16 knots. The larger ships of this type can carry 476 of the container units, each weighing up to 20 tons when loaded. Top photo shows how a container is raised from the trailer bed on the dock to the deck of the ship, or to a place atop other containers already in position. Crane operator rides in cab atop the frame, which grips top of container for lifting aboard ship. Photo on opposite page shows general view of this type ship with container trucks in line for loading (the first one with frame already attached is about to be raised) and containers already stacked on deck. Once the container is lifted, the huge crane (a part of ship) can move it to any position and lower it exactly in place. Note there are two of these moving cranes. The SS *Elizabethport* is an engine-aft type, and she has her bridge aft as well, for better container space forward.

Seatrain Georgia *(railway car and container carrier)*

One interesting way in which freight is moved from port to port is via the seatrain freighters operated by Seatrain Lines, Inc. These unique ships carry completely loaded freight cars on their decks on rails. The cars are lifted to the decks by gigantic hoists and then clamped in place on the deck, or belowdecks, on duplicate rails. At their destination the cars are removed by crane, set upon land tracks and hauled away by regular locomotives. This photo shows the *Seatrain Georgia,* 557 feet long with a beam of 63 feet. Her speed is 16 knots and she has a crew of 45. She has an engine-aft design, as you can see. On the opposite page (top) is an aerial view showing cars already loaded and more on the dock ready for lifting. These ships also carry 35-foot-long cargo containers which are land-transported on flatcars. The newer seatrains can carry 90 railroad cars and 72 containers. Diagram shows details of this ingenious operation.

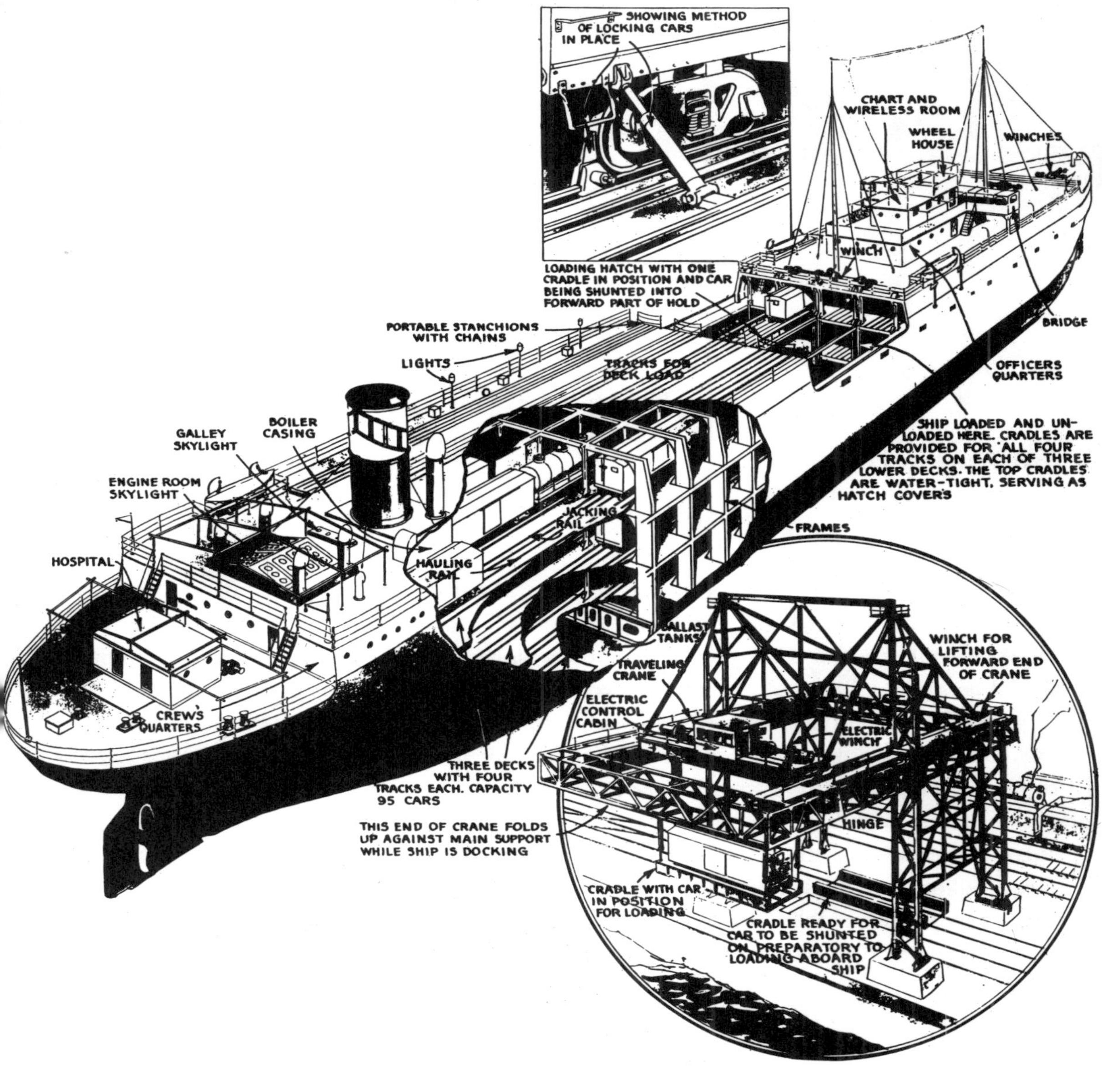

Labels (cutaway diagram):

- SHOWING METHOD OF LOCKING CARS IN PLACE
- LOADING HATCH WITH ONE CRADLE IN POSITION AND CAR BEING SHUNTED INTO FORWARD PART OF HOLD
- CHART AND WIRELESS ROOM
- WHEEL HOUSE
- WINCHES
- WINCH
- BRIDGE
- OFFICERS QUARTERS
- SHIP LOADED AND UNLOADED HERE. CRADLES ARE PROVIDED FOR EACH OF FOUR TRACKS ON EACH OF THREE LOWER DECKS. THE TOP CRADLES ARE WATER-TIGHT, SERVING AS HATCH COVERS
- PORTABLE STANCHIONS WITH CHAINS
- LIGHTS
- TRACKS FOR DECK LOAD
- FRAMES
- GALLEY SKYLIGHT
- BOILER CASING
- ENGINE ROOM SKYLIGHT
- JACKING RAIL
- HAULING RAIL
- HOSPITAL
- BALLAST TANKS
- TRAVELING CRANE
- ELECTRIC CONTROL CABIN
- CREW'S QUARTERS
- THREE DECKS WITH FOUR TRACKS EACH. CAPACITY 95 CARS
- THIS END OF CRANE FOLDS UP AGAINST MAIN SUPPORT WHILE SHIP IS DOCKING
- WINCH FOR LIFTING FORWARD END OF CRANE
- ELECTRIC WINCH
- HINGE
- CRADLE WITH CAR IN POSITION FOR LOADING
- CRADLE READY FOR CAR TO BE SHUNTED ON PREPARATORY TO LOADING ABOARD SHIP

M/V Harry Jefferies and J. E. Dyer
(oil tankers)

One of the most important ships of commerce is the oil tanker, upon which the world's machinery depends for fuel and lubricants. Moving their cargo from continent to continent is a huge undertaking, but such tankers as these help speed it on its way. Above, the M/V (motor vessel) *Harry Jefferies*, of the Sinclair Refining Company, with a length of 610 feet and a beam of 76 feet. She can carry 209,000 barrels of oil at a speed of 15 knots. She is one of the few "bridge-aft" tankers, and has a deadweight of 24,500 tons. On the opposite page (top) is another Sinclair tanker, the *J. E. Dyer*. She is even larger but has her bridge forward. Both ships have their engines aft. The *J. E. Dyer* is 661 feet long with a beam of 90 feet and a speed of 16 knots, a bit faster than the *Harry Jefferies*. She can carry 271,000 barrels of oil. The lower photo shows an oil barge pulled by a tug, a means of moving bulk oil about a harbor for fueling ships, and moving it to shoreline consumers. The barges are divided into compartments, and powerful pumps are used to move oil from the barge to the consumer. Square ends of barges permit pushing several in a row or lashing them together for towing.

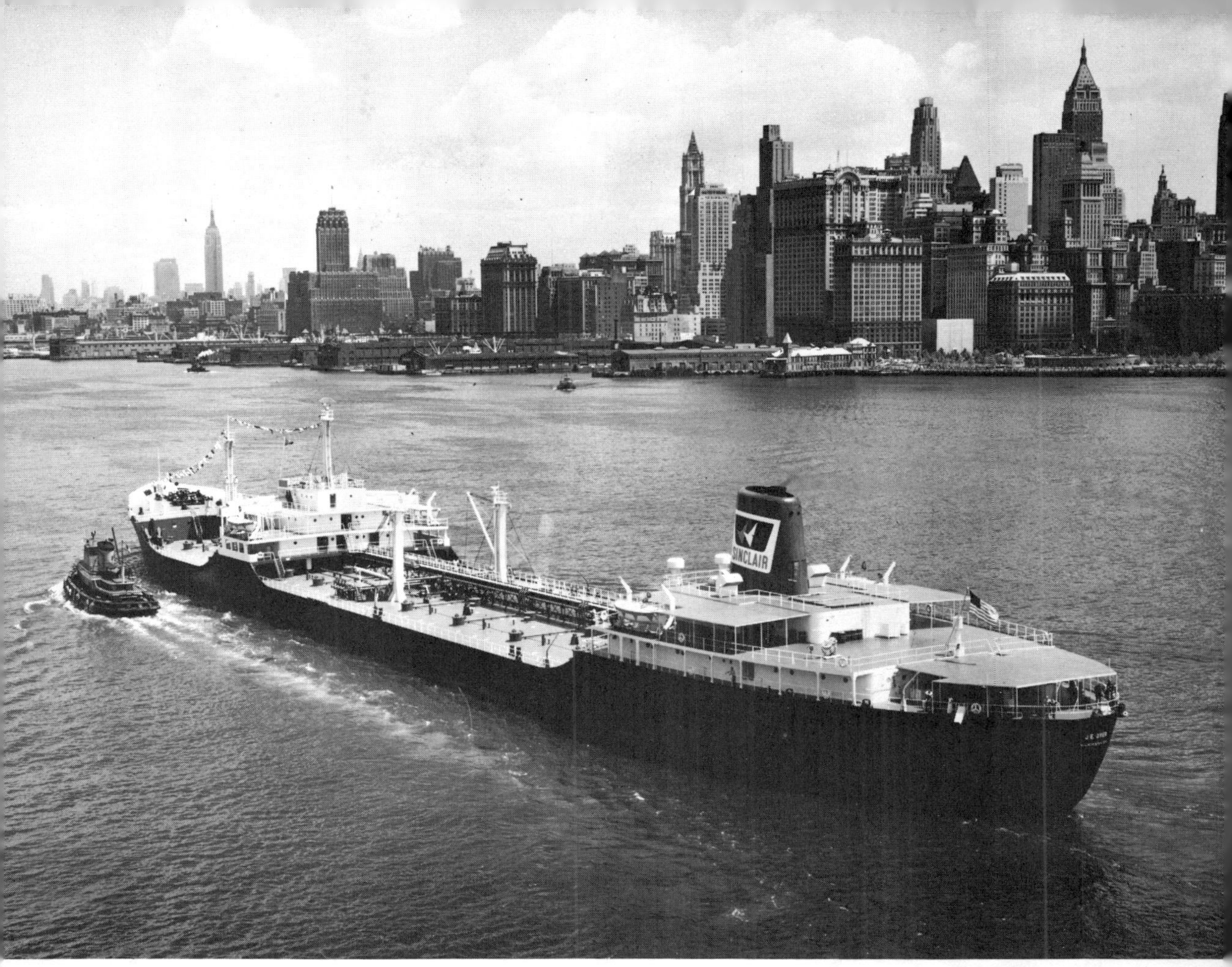
SINCLAIR

OIL TRANSFER NO. 25 WILMINGTON DEL.

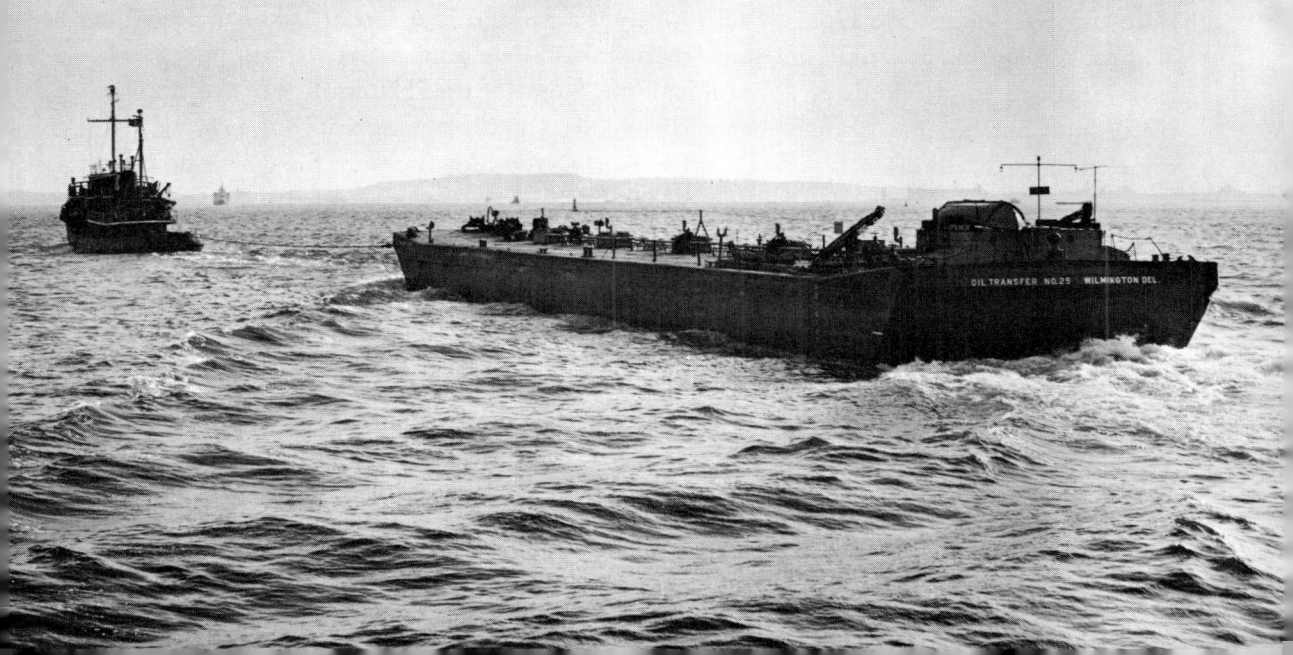

Amoco Wisconsin and SS Meadowbrook
(oil tankers)

Here are two interesting types of oil tankers. At the top is a Great Lakes tanker, the *Amoco Wisconsin*, operated by the American Oil Company, which transports petroleum products to terminals on lakes Michigan, Superior and Huron. It is of the engine-aft design, but has the bridge in the extreme bow in direct contrast to the *Harry Jefferies* on page 30. Below this "laker" is the giant SS *Meadowbrook* of the Keystone Shipping Co. This tanker, with the bridge amidships and the engines aft, is 606 feet long with a beam of 80 feet. This photo is interesting in that it shows the tanker very lightly loaded with most of the hull above-water. If she were loaded, most of the lighter-colored sides would be below the waterline. Each vessel of any type is marked for safe loading under various conditions, and these limits must be strictly observed as to summer, winter, and, in some instances, where the ship is to travel. On the opposite page is a fine view of another vessel of the American Oil Company, the *Amoco Missouri* towboat, pushing a string of oil barges through a canal lock on the Mississippi River. These barges are flush deck without crew quarters. (For description of towboats, see page 42.)

SS *Cobetas* (grain carrier) and Floating Grain Elevators

The handling of grain requires ships designed for that purpose, and also such odd craft as floating elevators. At the top of this page is a view of floating grain elevators in use. They are the two tall structures on the hulls between the barges and the grain carrier ship by the dockside. Since some ships can carry both grain and other cargo, while the regular cargo is being loaded from the dock the grain is being loaded from the floating elevators on the other side. The forward grain elevator is the *America*, a self-propelled vessel. There are also nonself-propelled floating elevators which are moved by tug. The grain is loaded into these unique ships from barges and then transferred by high pipes into the holds of the ships. Floating grain elevators can handle as much as 20,000 bushels of grain an hour. On the opposite page is a view of the SS *Cobetas*, taking on grain from a dock elevator via the long discharging pipes leading into the holds.

Albatross IV, George M. Bowers, and M/V Delaware (fishing research)

Fishing boats of all kinds are important to commerce, and even more important are the boats used for fishing research. Here are three fishing vessels of the Fish and Wildlife Service of the U. S. Department of the Interior, used for commercial fishing research. At the top is the *Albatross IV*, a 187-foot, single-screw stern trawler, used to chart distribution and abundance of groundfish and scallops, and to carry out other research. The stern ramp permits hauling loaded nets even during heavy weather. She has underwater television, laboratories and every facility for deepwater research. She has a speed of 12 knots and a range of over 9,000 miles. She is completely air-conditioned and can be used in arctic as well as tropic waters. She carries a crew of 22 and 16 scientists. On opposite page (top) is the motor vessel *George M. Bowers*, a typical shrimp trawler, used by the U. S. Bureau of Commercial Fisheries for research. There are about 5,000 of these shrimp trawlers used by the shrimp industry in the southeast. This ship is used in the Gulf of Mexico, and is 73 feet long with a beam of 21 feet. She has a maximum speed of 10 knots and carries a crew of six, plus four scientists. Special research equipment has been added. Opposite (bottom) is shown the motor vessel *Delaware*, also of the Bureau of Commercial Fisheries. This 138-foot research vessel has a beam of 25 feet and a speed of 10 knots. She carries a crew of 23, plus scientists, and is used in many types of commercial fishing research.

John N. Cobb, Oregon and Kaho
(fishing research)

In the Pacific Northwest and Alaska, fishing is a main industry, and the U. S. Fish and Wildlife Service uses these vessels there for research and exploration. At the top is the *John N. Cobb*, a specially equipped, West Coast purse seiner, with a length of 93 feet and a beam of 85 feet. She has a speed of 10 knots and can carry a crew of 10, plus 4 scientists. Much scientific equipment is aboard to aid in research on the tuna-fishing industry in particular. On the opposite page (top) is a photo of the *Oregon*, a tuna-fishing vessel now used in the Gulf of Mexico. She is a converted West Coast tuna bait boat equipped with research gear to help the shrimp fishermen locate and commercialize new species of shrimp. At the bottom is the 65-foot *Kaho* (Chippewa Indian word for "hunt"), with a speed of 10 knots. She is equipped with fishing research instruments to make profile records of the sea bottom as well as schools of fish. She carries a crew of 4, plus scientific personnel. All of these fishing research vessels carry radio and/or radio phones; in many cases, radar and various types of nets, seines and other standard fishing equipment.

Diana L. Moran (tugboat)

The harbors of the world would be a lot less efficient were it not for the small but powerful tugboats, forever pushing, shoving and towing everything from garbage scows to luxury liners. The biggest tug operator is the Moran Towing and Transportation Company, operator of 30 of these powerful vessels. At the top is a fine aerial view of two tugs docking a liner, and on the opposite page are two views of the *Diana L. Moran*, a typical, seagoing tug of this fleet. She is 106 feet long with a beam of 27 feet. Her speed averages about 14 knots, but is governed by type of work. She is a world-wide tug and can tow almost any load across the ocean or to any point on the globe. She carries 32,000 gallons of fuel and has a crew of twelve. There are smaller and larger tugs in this fleet, each designed for efficient towing or shoving. The ragged-looking objects hanging over the sides and massed on the bow of this tug are rope bumpers to protect the tug, as well as the vessel being maneuvered, from damage. Tugs of this type carry most modern navigation instruments, including radar, radio phones and some fire-fighting equipment. They are fine deepwater vessels, powerful and dependable and very seaworthy, even when towing. Note huge coils of towlines on aft deck of *Diana L. Moran*.

United States, Philip Sporn and Patrick Calhoun, Jr. (towboats)

Much of our big-river commercial traffic is handled by "towboats," as they are called, although they usually push their barges rather than tow them as they did in the old days. These highly specialized motor vessels are designed with square bows, equipped with rugged vertical units to push against the backs of barges or groups of barges. At the top is shown the United States of the Federal Barge Lines, Inc., pushing 35 big barges on the Mississippi River. The cargo on these loaded barges includes: wine, carbon-black steel, sugar, sulphur, oyster shells, molasses, superphosphate, pulp paper and contractors' equipment, all destined for ports up the river. The United States, also shown top of opposite page, is equipped with the latest in river-navigation instruments, radar, radio, and carries a crew of about 22. Opposite page (center) shows the Philip Sporn, of the American Barge Line Company. Below is her larger sister ship, the Patrick Calhoun, Jr. Both ships were built by Jefferson Boat and Machine Co., and the Patrick Calhoun, Jr. was their 1,000th hull. She is one of the largest river towboats ever built. Her length is 190 feet, her beam 48 feet and she can push a string of barges as much as a third of a mile long with 40,000 tons of cargo. She carries a crew of around 25 and is equipped with an automatic pilot system, two radars, carbon-arc searchlights, and two radiophone systems, plus automatic depth sounder. Crew quarters are air-conditioned, and she has a strictly modern kitchen with a dishwasher.

Dredges

Sooner or later, almost every navigable river, canal or harbor requires the expert services of some sort of dredge to widen, deepen or clear the channel. There are six basic types of dredges, all designed to do one thing — dig up the bottom of the waterway and move it elsewhere. At the top of page is the *Frontera I*, a hopper dredge. This "ship" is 186 feet long with a beam of 35 feet. Powerful pumps operate a suction pipe reaching downward from the bottom of the hull. This sucks up the channel bottom and deposits it in huge hoppers aboard the vessel. These hoppers hold many tons of "slurry," as the mixture of water and mud and rock is called. When the hoppers are filled, the vessel steams out into deep water where the hydraulically operated lower doors of the hoppers are opened and the contents dumped; then back for another load. She has a speed of 10 knots when hoppers are full and over 11 knots when they are empty. On the opposite page (top) is the *Hydro-Quebec*, a hydraulic pipeline cutterhead dredge. These operate via a long suction pipe with a rotating cutterhead on the end to break up the hard bottom clays. This giant can break up and remove hardest types of glacial boulder clays and handle boulders up to almost a ton in weight. It is used on the St. Lawrence Seaway. It is operated by electricity and can dig to a depth of 50 feet. Removed material is pumped ashore via floating pipeline. Lower photo shows a dipper dredge, a sort of floating steamshovel which removes bottom material and loads onto barges alongside or ashore. All these models plus others are built and designed by Ellicott Machine Corp.

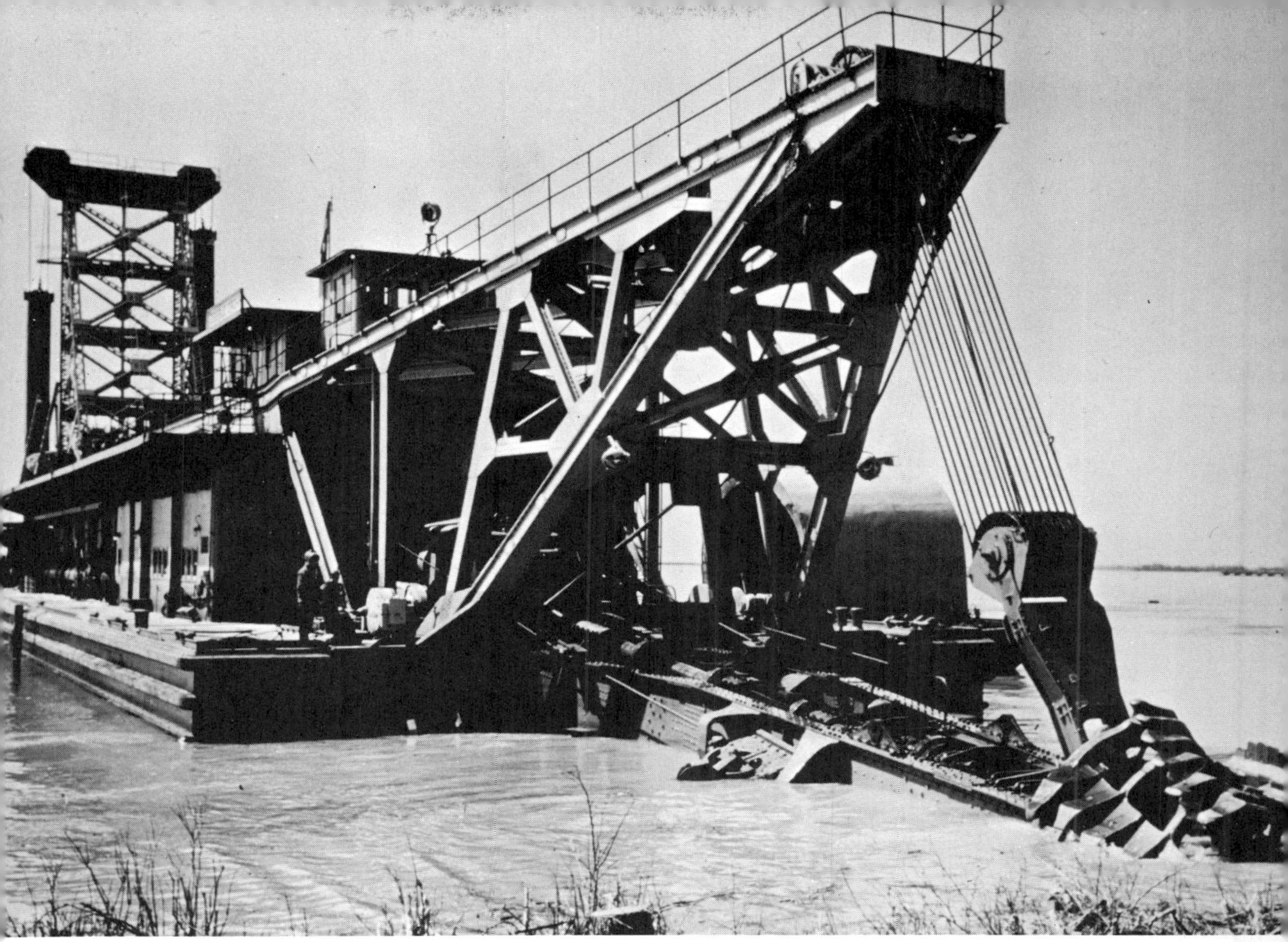

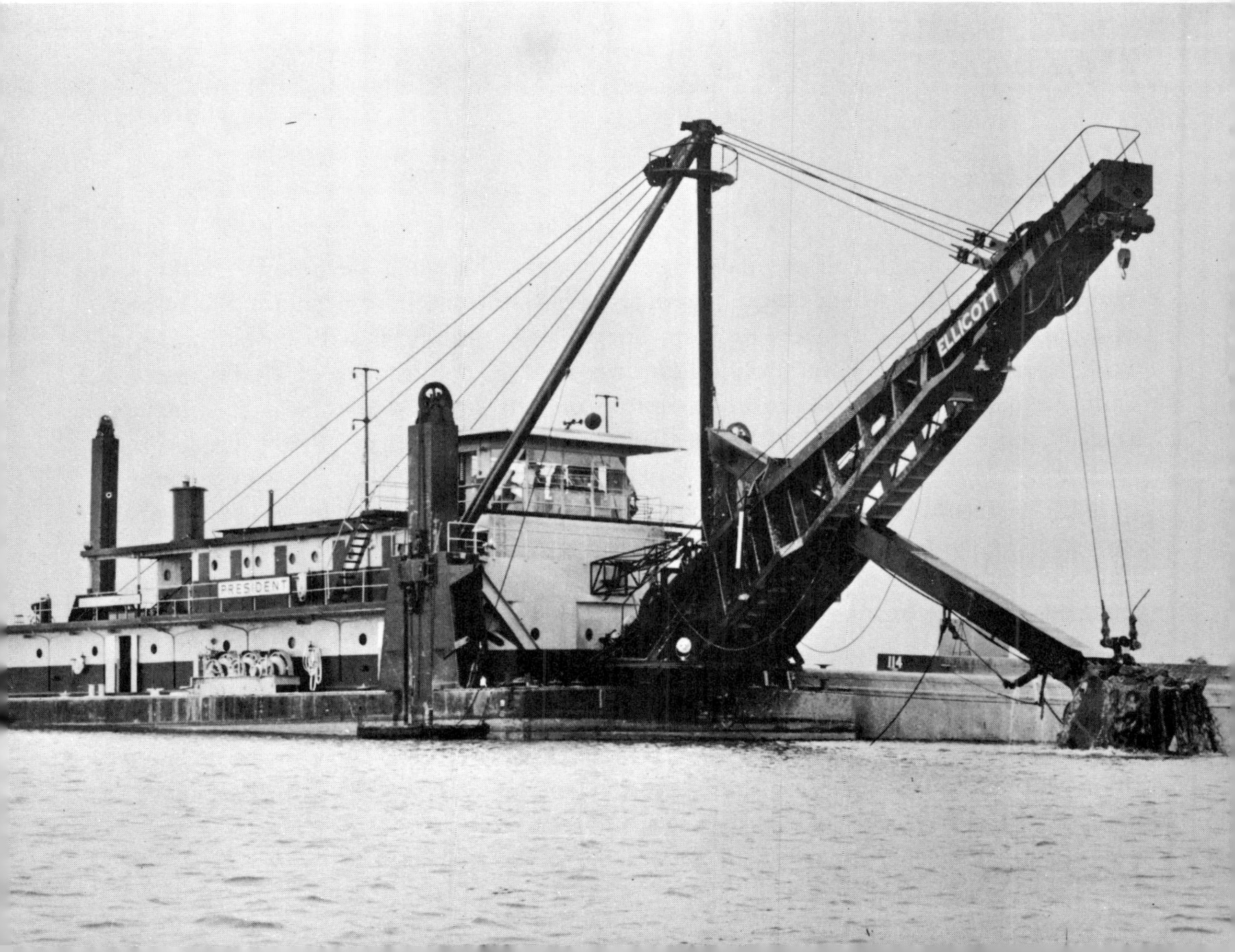
ELLICOTT
PRESIDENT
114

Barges

Every large harbor is full of many types of boats, ships and barges. The latter are especially important where cargoes have to be moved from shore to shore, pier to pier, or from ship to shore or shore to ship. Barges vary greatly in size, design and purpose. Here are several different types of barges. At the top is a tug of the Baltimore & Ohio Railroad, moving two railroad barges or "car floats" across New York harbor. Each barge is equipped with standard rails and can carry up to 18 fully loaded railroad cars. On the opposite page (top) an oil barge of the Sinclair Refining Company is pushed up a river by a small towboat. This oil barge can carry up to 12 separate grades for a total of 19,000 barrels in one load. Photo in center is a tug of the Erie Railroad, moving three flush-deck barges. Note the crated tractors and graders on front barge. Some barges have cabins for barge captains in case of bad weather. Bottom photo shows tug of Pennsylvania Railroad with three barges, two of which are covered. These can be loaded through roof hatches or doors. On page 48 a string of ten barges loaded with gravel and building materials is being towed by a tug assisted by a second tug. Note how the gravel has been evenly loaded and shaped to prevent shifting and perhaps capsizing the barges. When next you visit a big harbor, see how many of these ships, barges and tugs you can recognize.

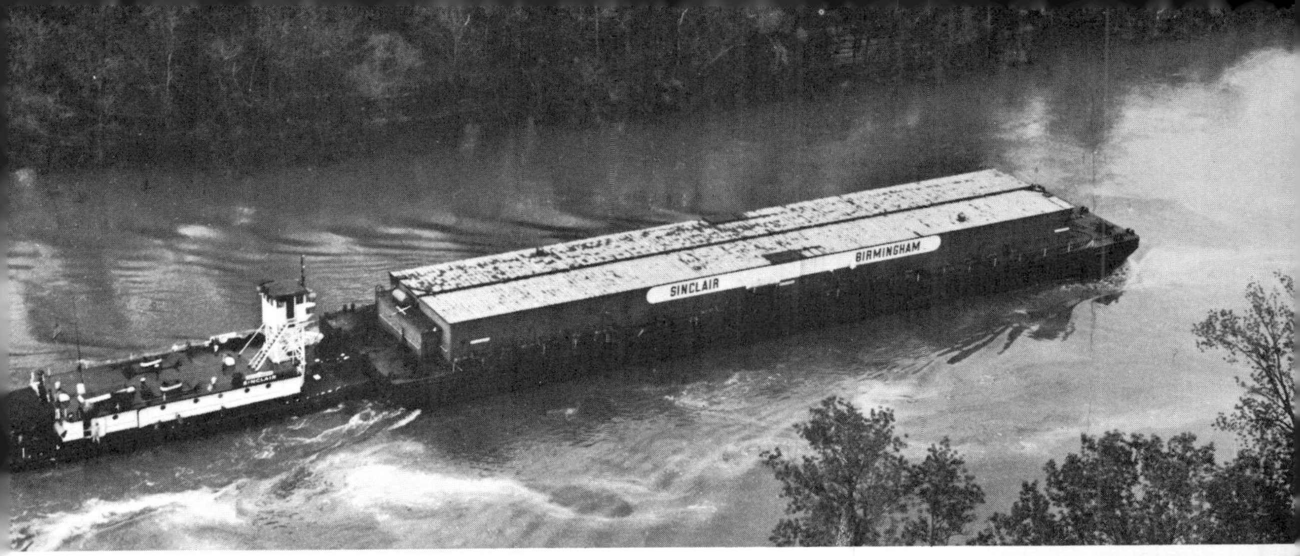
SINCLAIR
BIRMINGHAM

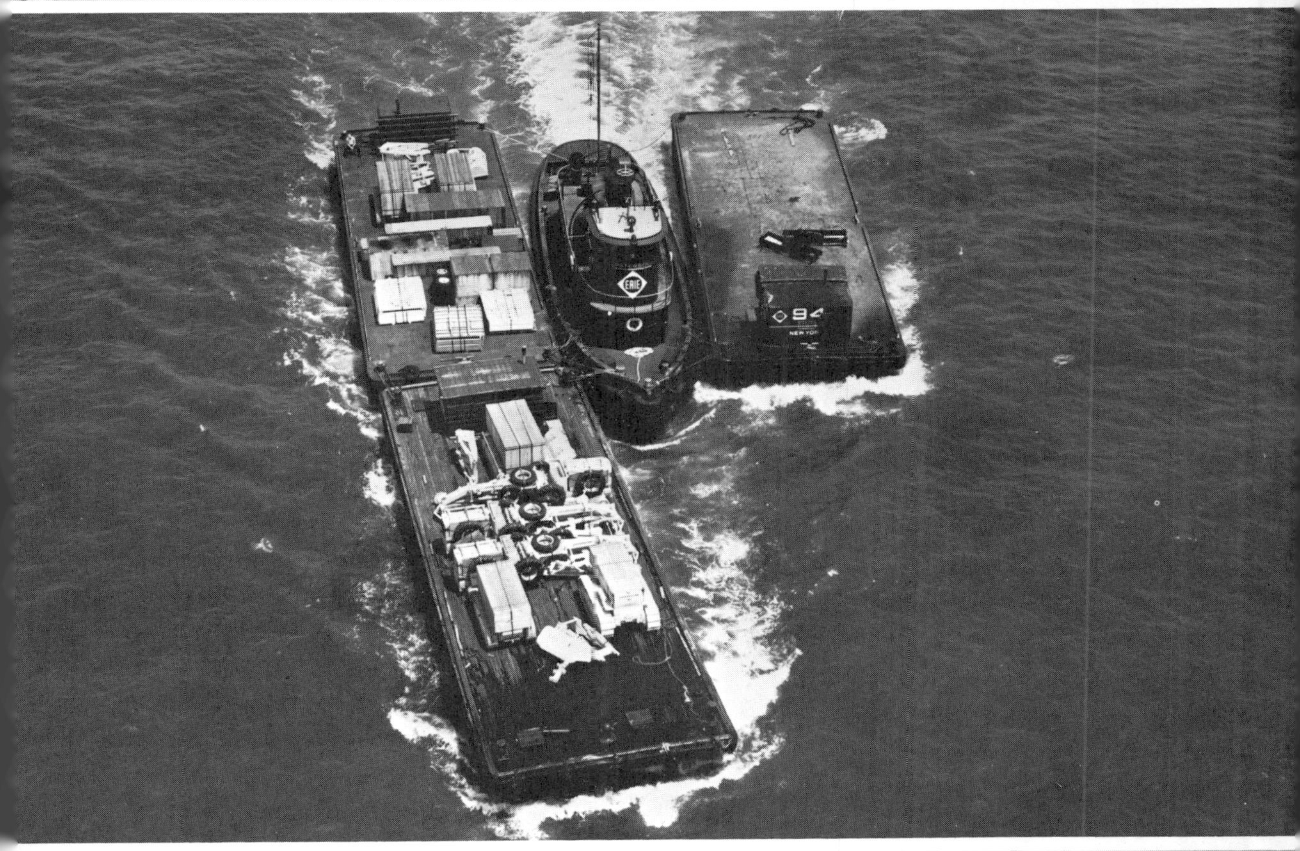
ERIE
94

409
395

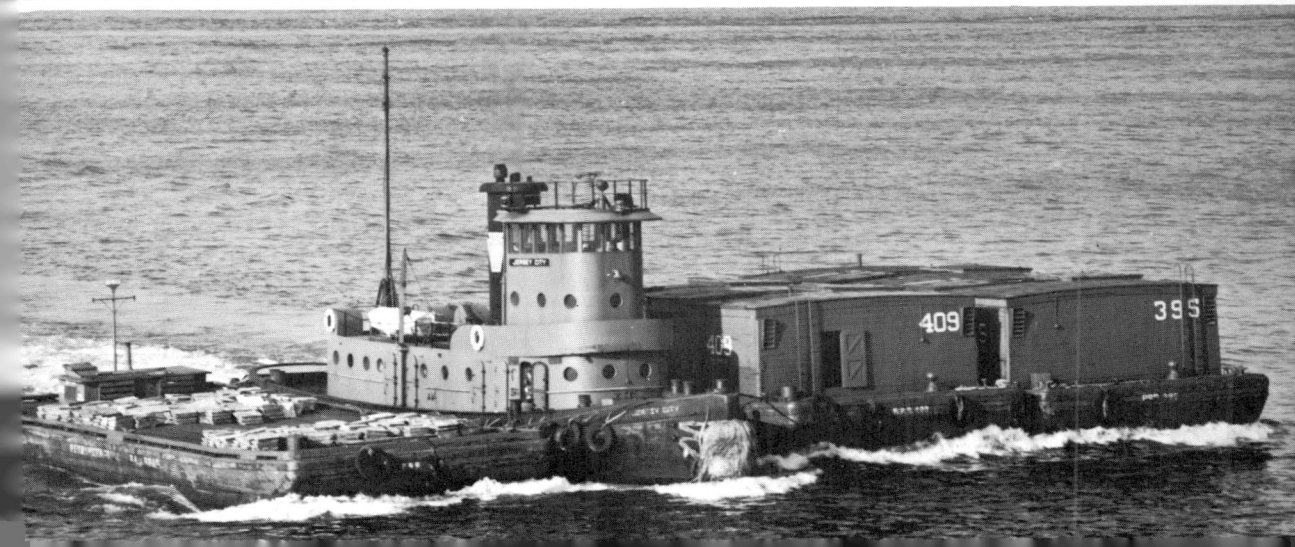

2578